ISHA UPANISHAD

Om shanti shanti shanti

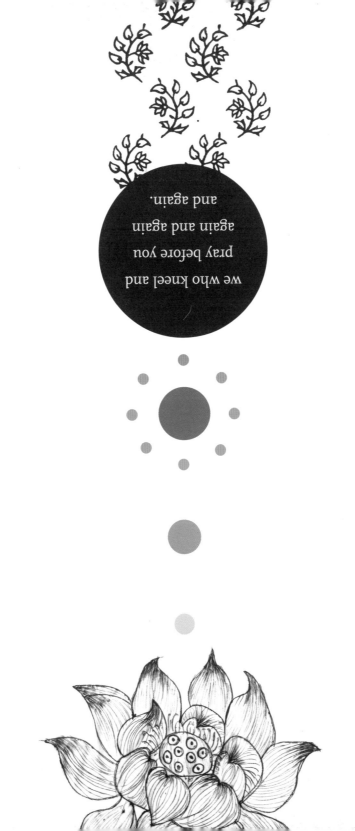

we who kneel and
pray before you
again and again
and again.

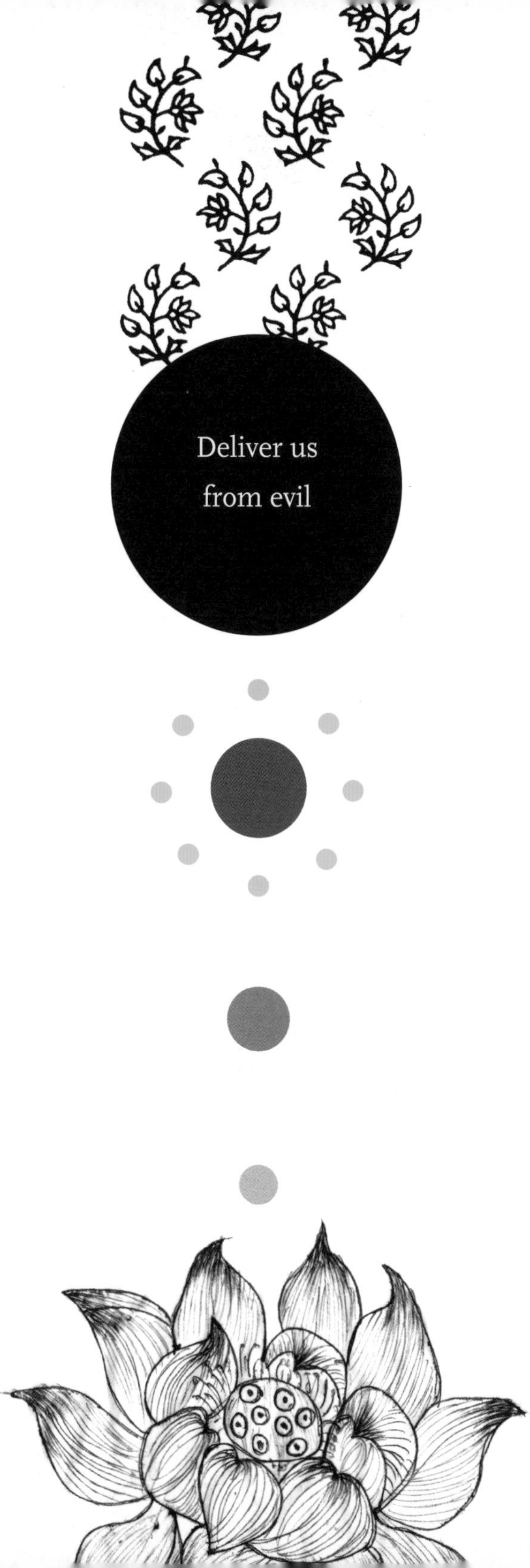
Deliver us
from evil

You know everything
we have done.

O God of Fire,
walk us down the path
of goodness
to eternal joy.

Remember,
O Mind, everything
that happened.

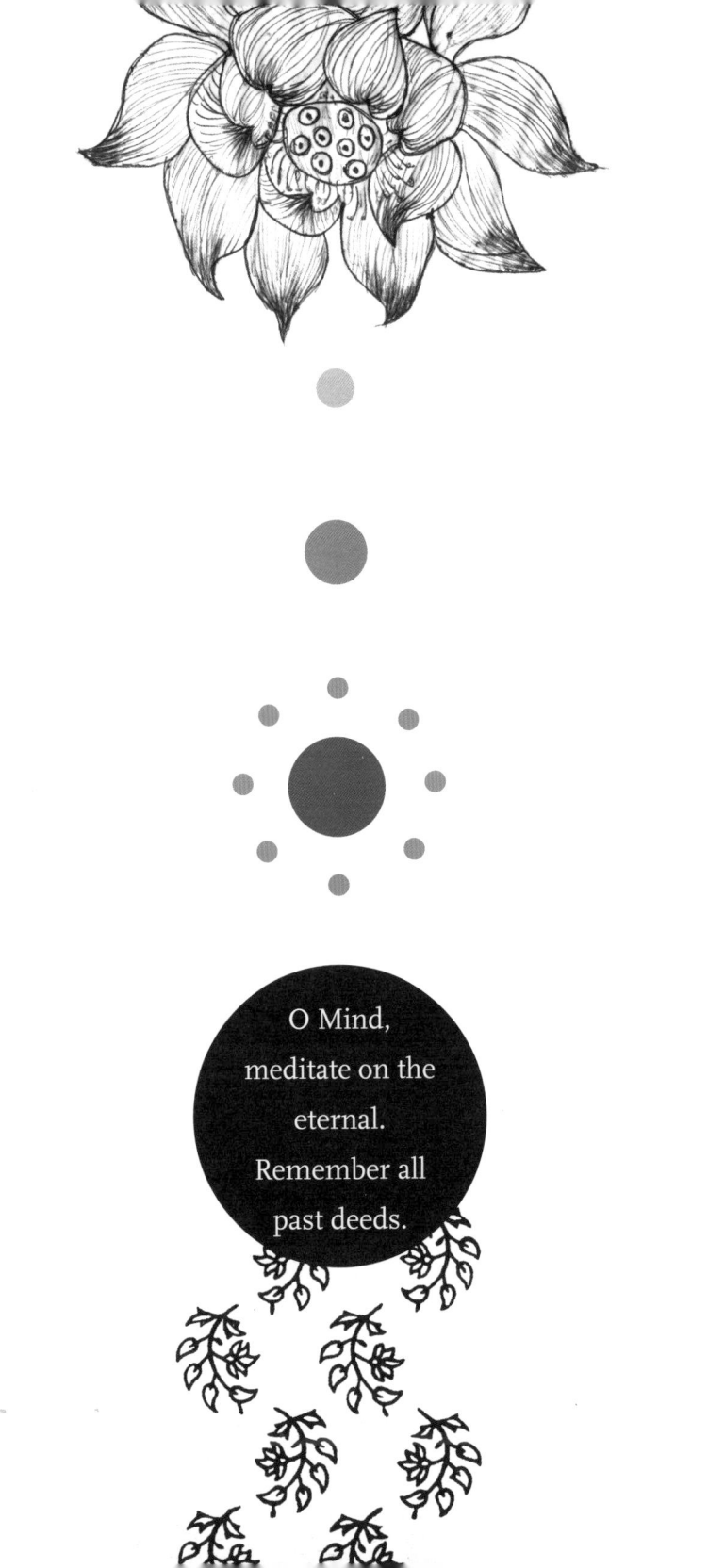

O Mind,
meditate on the
eternal.
Remember all
past deeds.

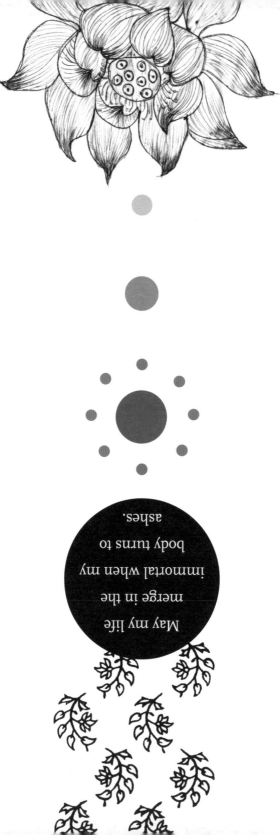

May my life
merge in the
immortal when my
body turns to
ashes.

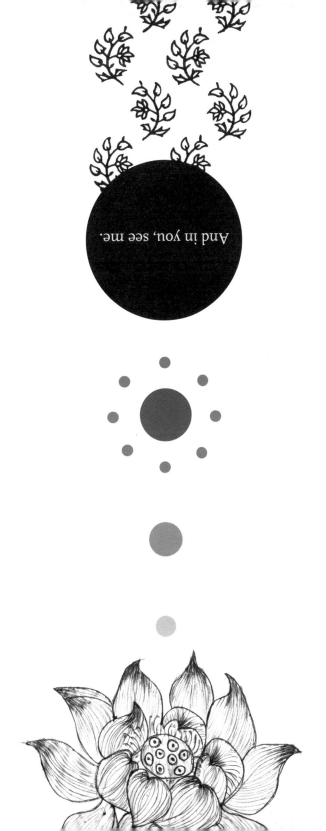

And in you, see me.

subdue your
resplendence
so that I
may see you.

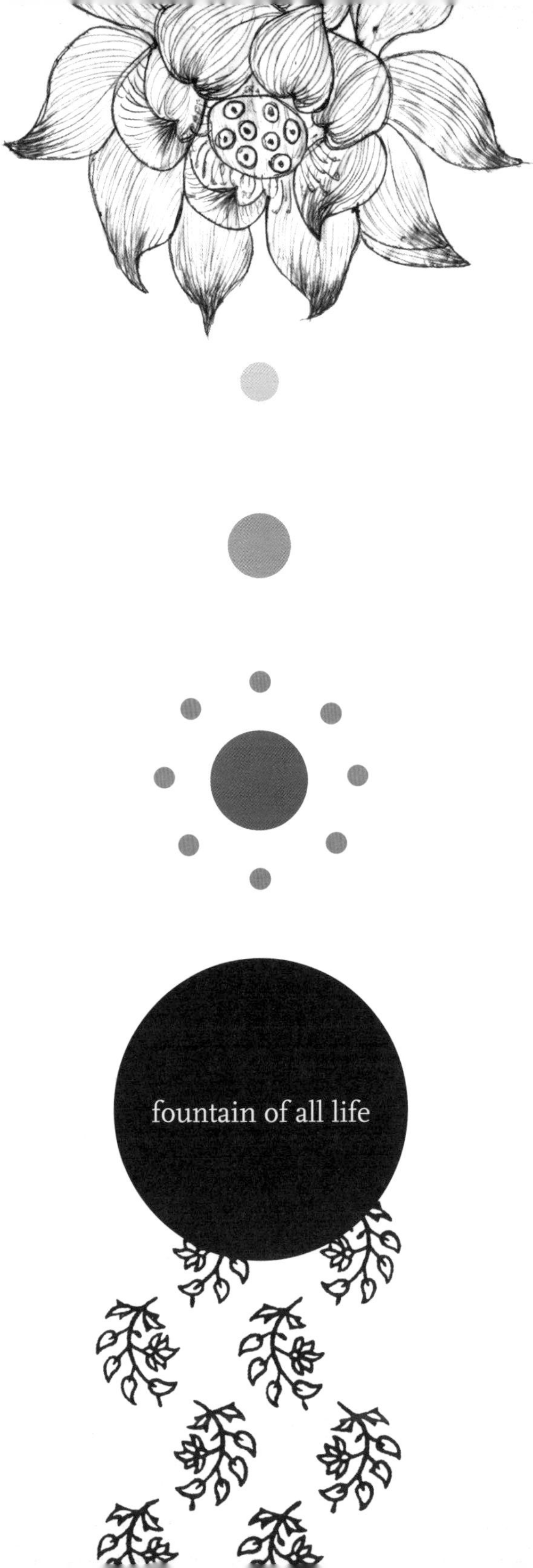
fountain of all life

O all-nurturing
Sun, solitary
journeyman,
He who controls
all things,

Move it, so that
I who worship
the truth may see
its true glory.

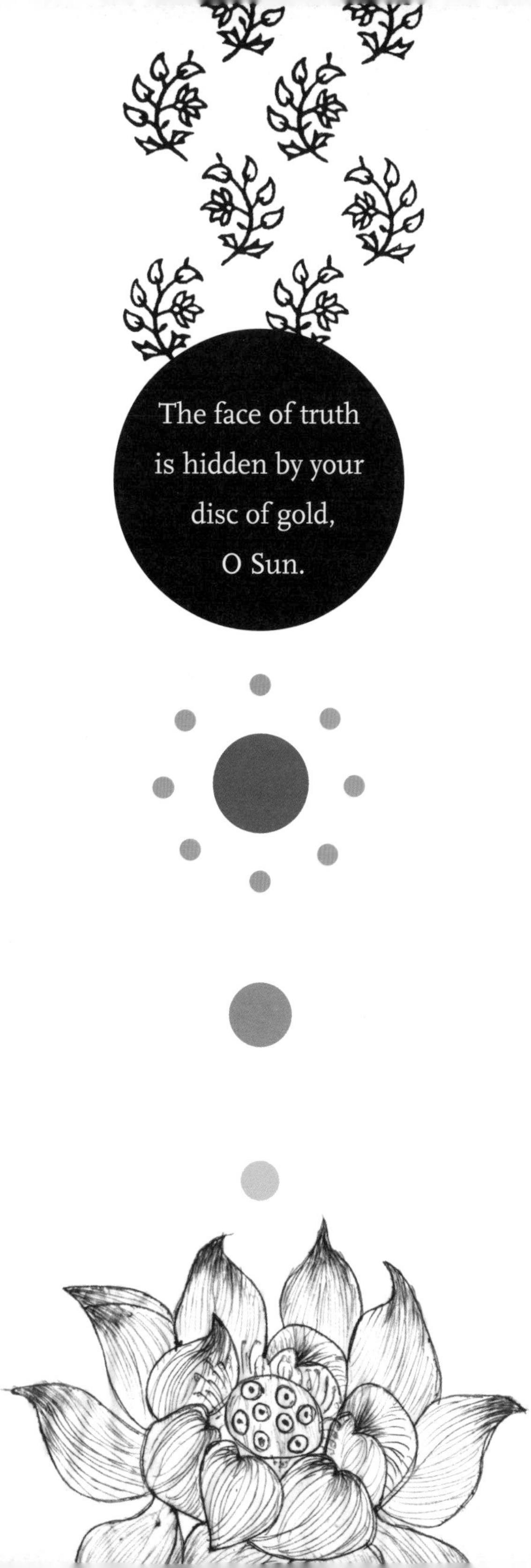
The face of truth
is hidden by your
disc of gold,
O Sun.

and enter
immortality.
Or so we have heard
from the wise.

Those for
whom he is both
transcendent and
immanent
cross the sea of
death

In the darker
night live those
for whom
He is immanent.

In the dark night
live those for whom
He is transcendent.

will cross the sea of
death and attain
immortality.

action

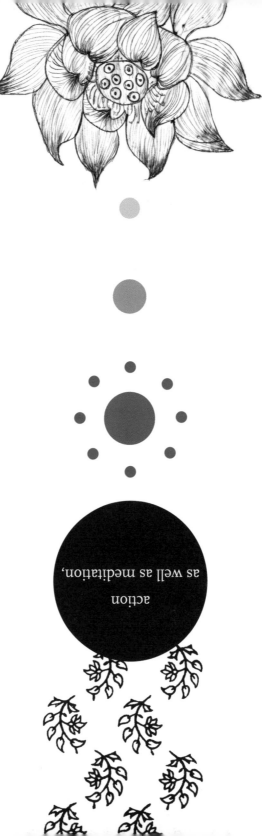

as well as meditation,

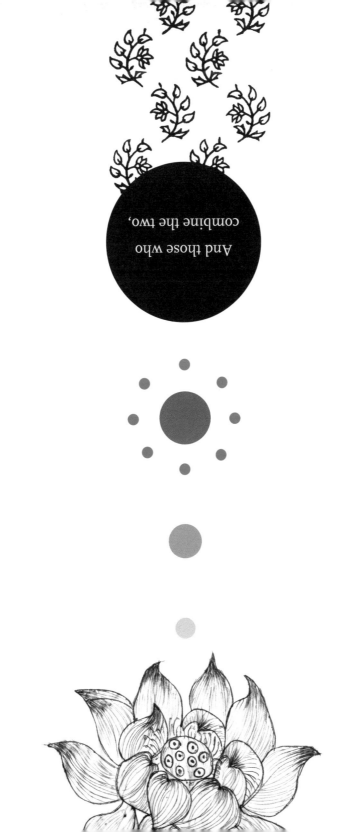

And those who
combine the two,

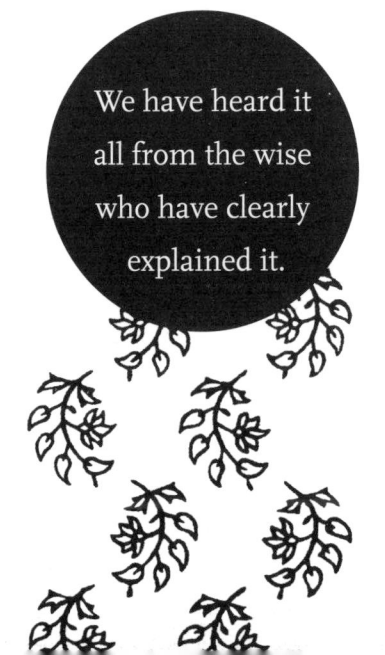

We have heard it
all from the wise
who have clearly
explained it.

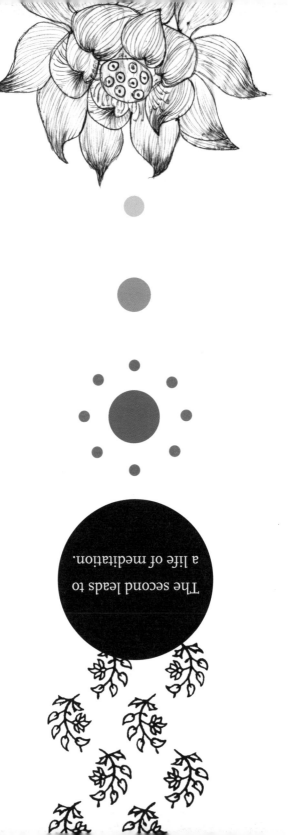

The second leads to
a life of meditation.

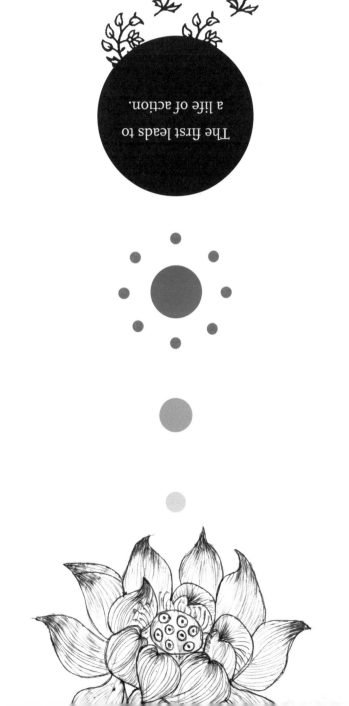

The first leads to
a life of action.

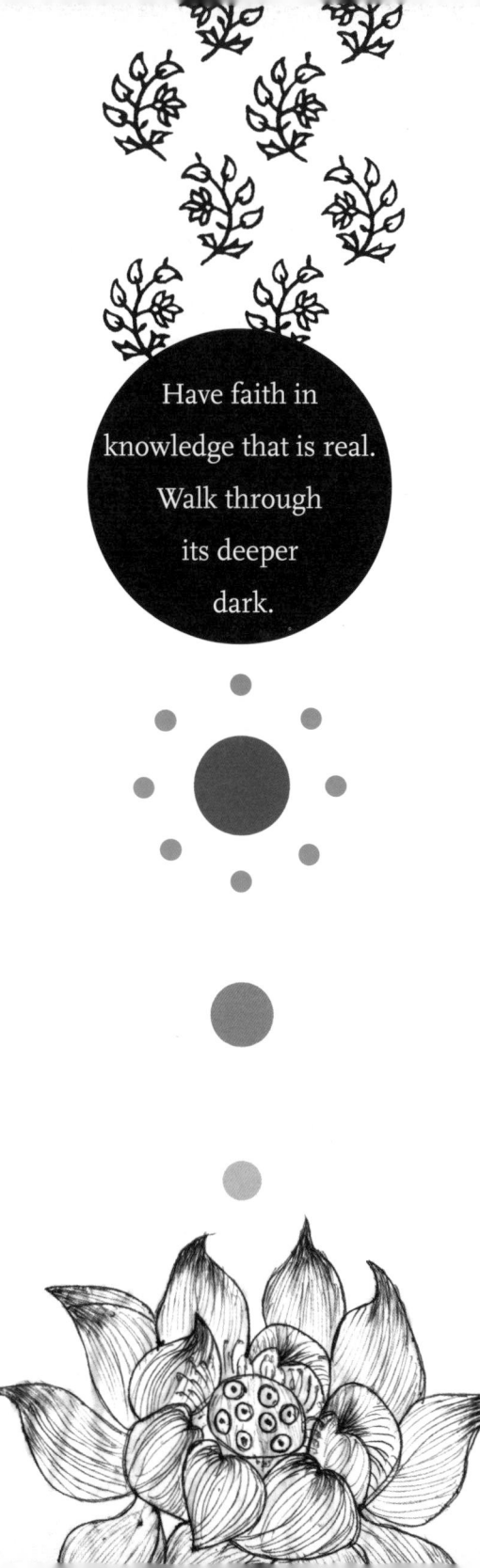

Have faith in
knowledge that is real.
Walk through
its deeper
dark.

Have faith in
knowledge that is real.
Walk through its
blinding
darkness.

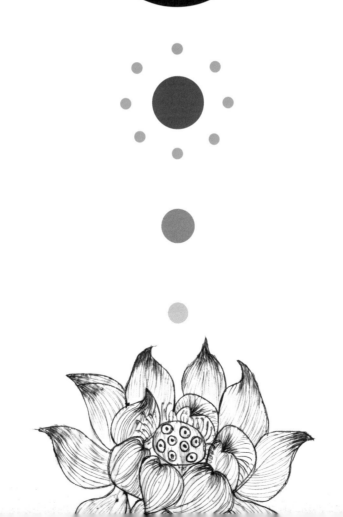

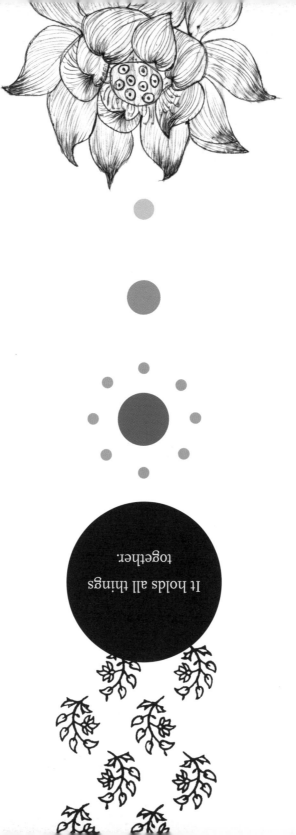

It holds all things
together.

It is
all knowing,
immanent,
transcendent.

It is without
body, shape,
untouched by sin,
wise.

The Self
is everywhere,
in everything.

How can life
delude the one who
sees its vastness
and its oneness?

and themselves
in all creatures
know no grief
either.

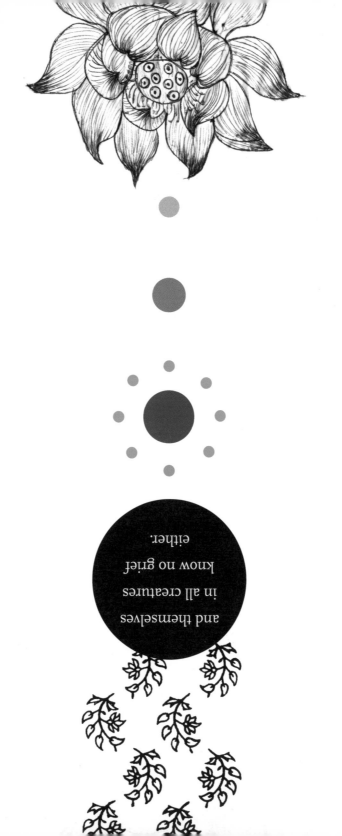

Those
who see
all creatures
in themselves

and themselves in
all creatures
know no fear.

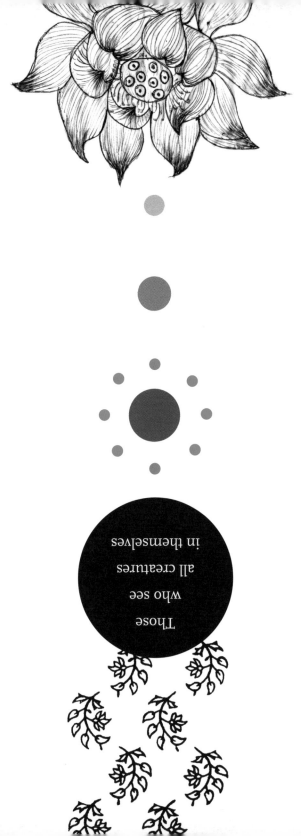

Those
who see
all creatures
in themselves

Yet

it

transcends

everything.

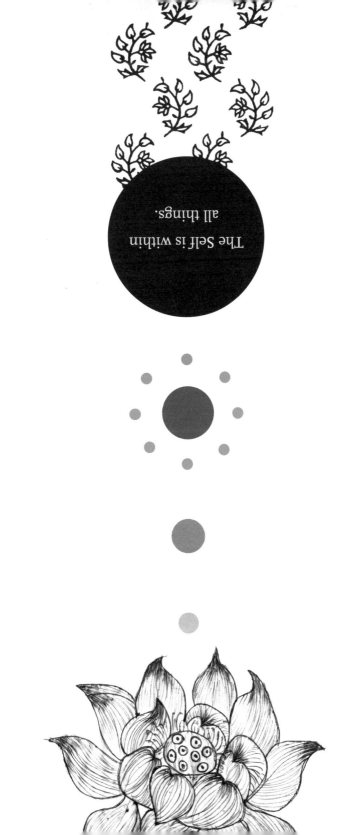

The Self is within
all things.

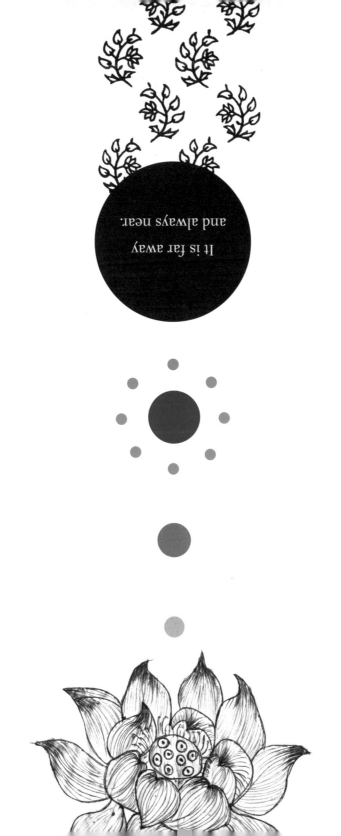

It is far away
and always near.

It moves
but is always still.

Without the Self,
life will not exist.

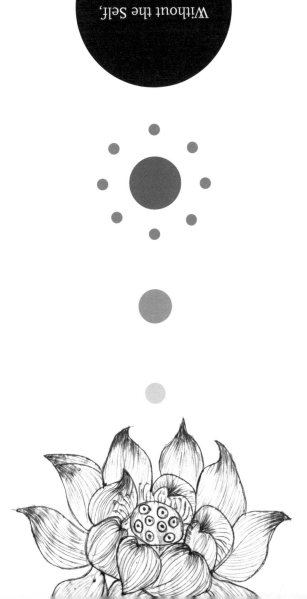

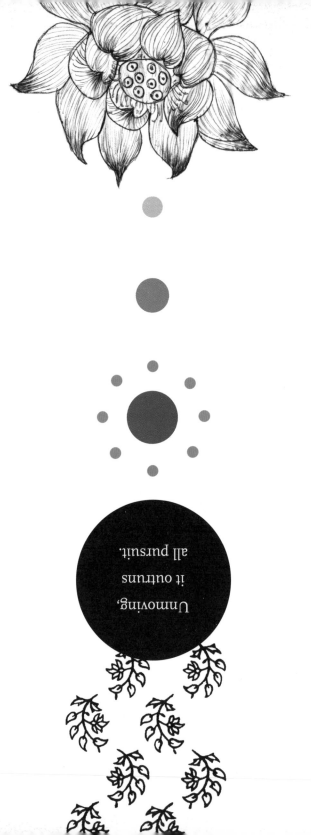

Unmoving,
it outruns
all pursuit.

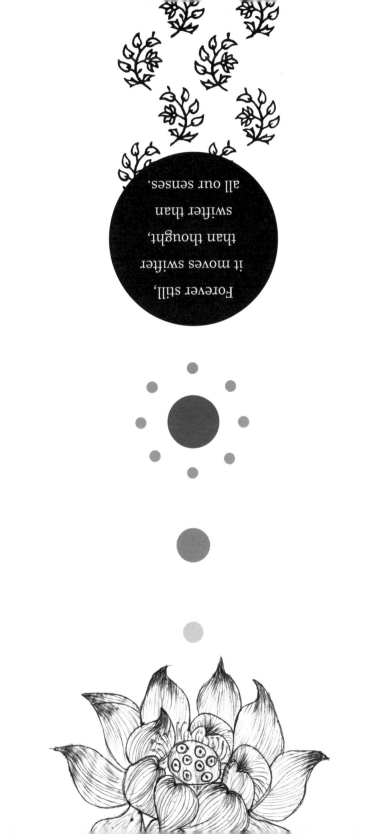

Forever still,
it moves swifter
than thought,
swifter than
all our senses.

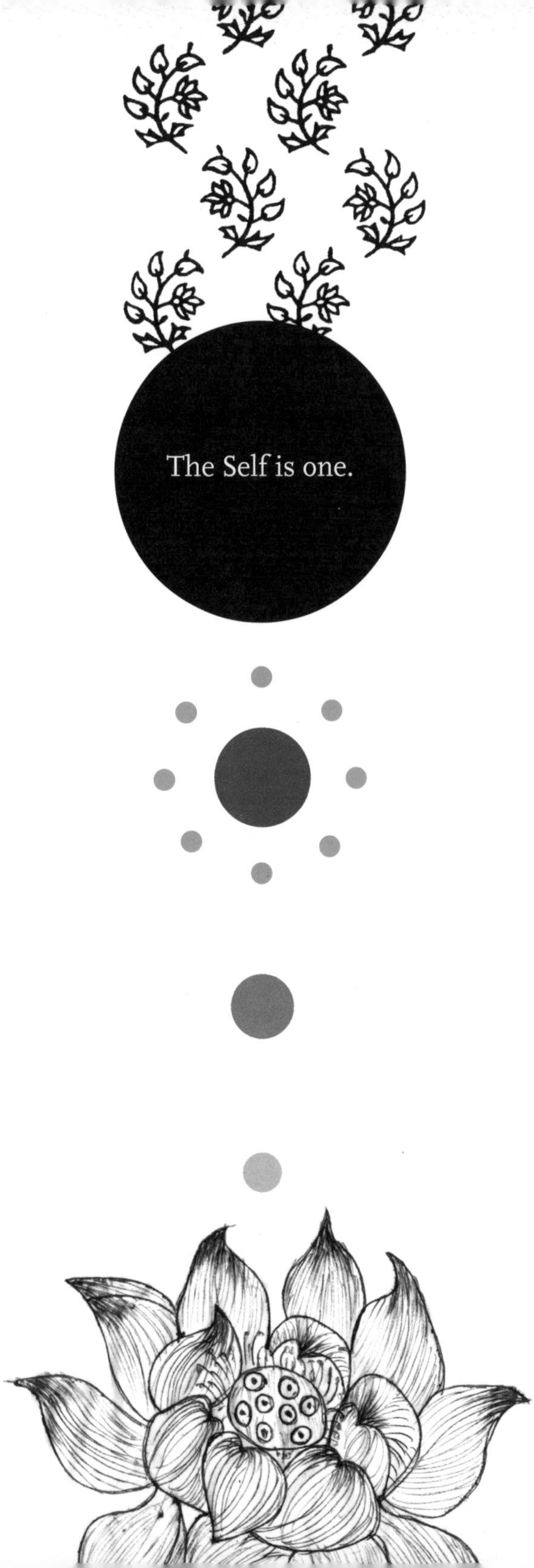
The Self is one.

All those who
spurn the Self in their
lifetime are drawn
towards the darkness
of death.

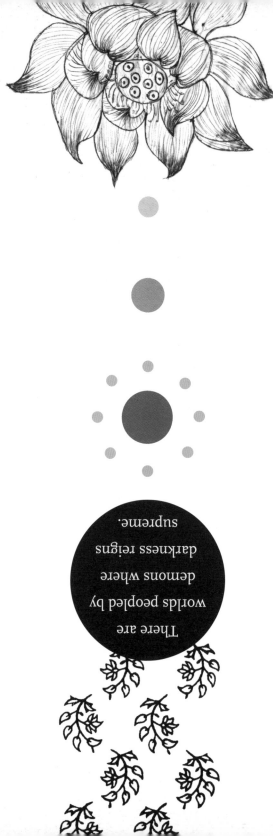

There are
worlds peopled by
demons where
darkness reigns
supreme.

Through acts
committed in
His name.
And no, not
otherwise.

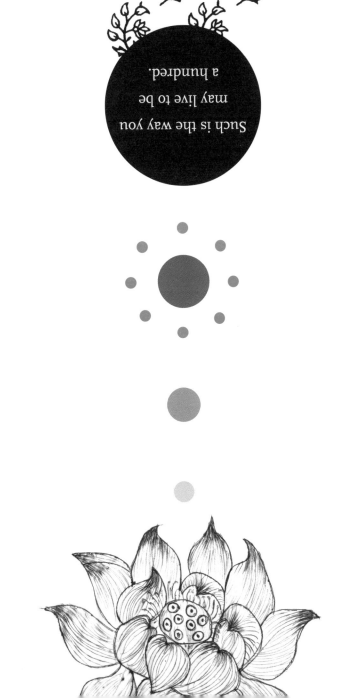

Such is the way you
may live to be
a hundred.

Covet not
what belongs
to others.

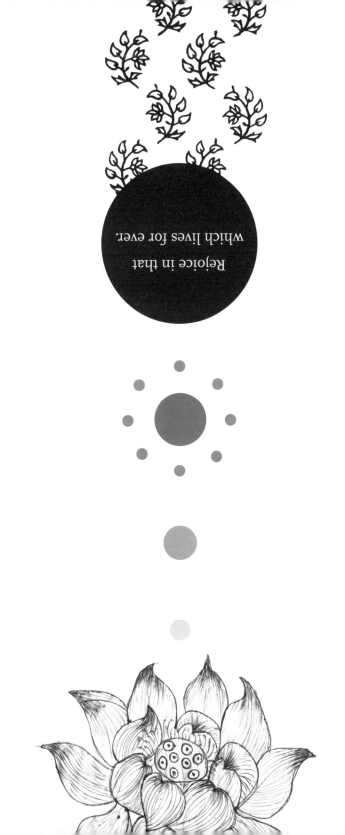

Rejoice in that
which lives for ever.

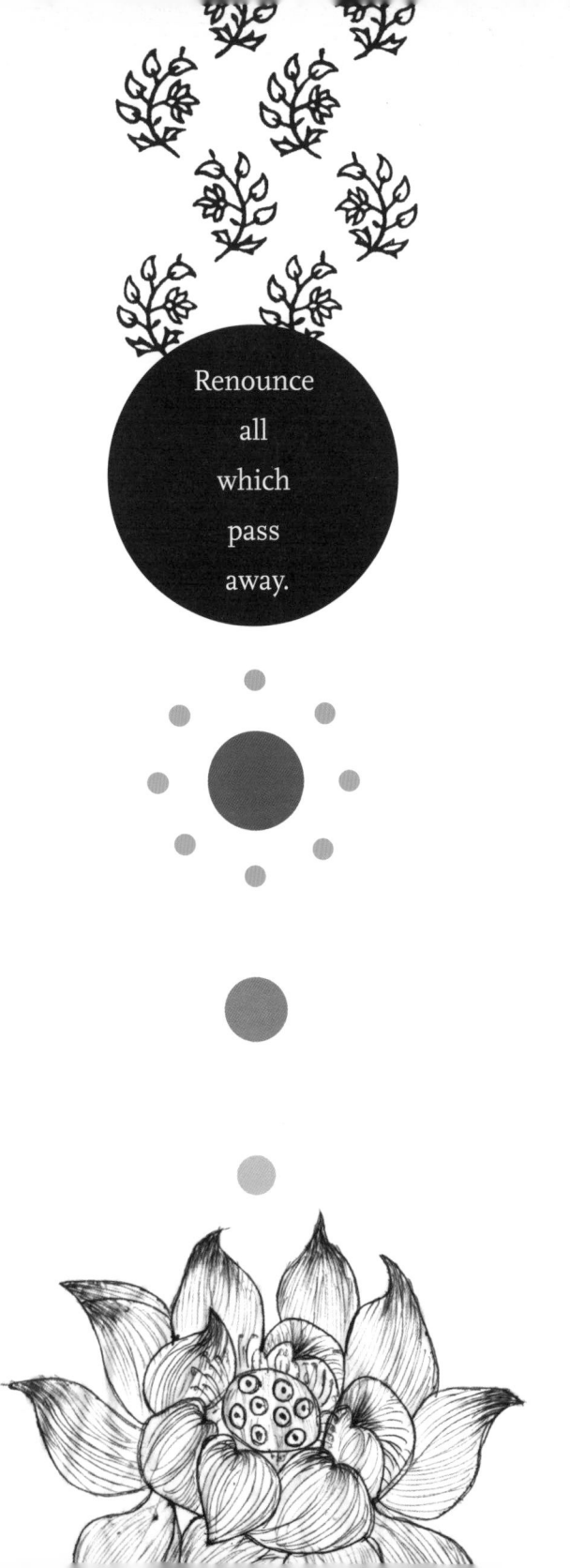

Renounce
all
which
pass
away.

He exists
in all that lives.

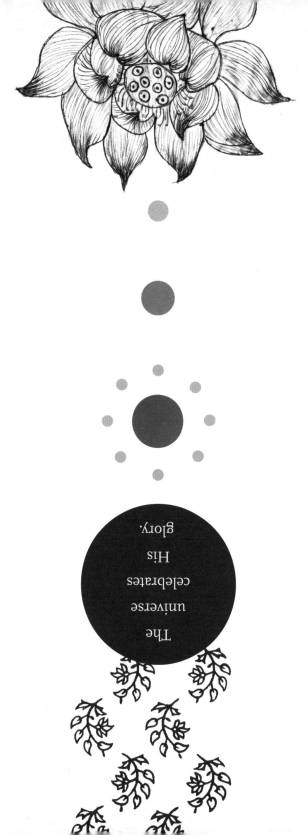

The
universe
celebrates
His
glory.

Om shanti shanti shanti

That is full.
This is full.

From the full
comes the full.

Remove the full
from the full
and what remains?

The full.

while doing so, ended up doing a fresh translation. That's when I realized how much language has changed over the past 35 years—how much I have changed. This version of the Isha, my favourite Upanishad, is infinitely simpler now in this incarnation and that is how—I believe today—it ought to be.

When I have a manuscript like this, there is only one publisher I think of. So I promptly mailed it to my friend Naveen Kishore and he, in turn, passed it on to Sunandini Banerjee who created these wonderfully illuminated illustrations. Together, I would like to believe, they may provide you a fascinating insight into the magic, the mystery and the incredible eloquence of what Mahatma Gandhi once famously described as the most important of all our scriptures. The one book that could outlive all the rest. The Isha Upanishad.

No, I must confess, diving deep into the Isha did not change my life as it did to many of my more famous predecessors. But who knows, it could change yours. In its incredible wisdom lies amazing power, and a rare insight into what makes our life whole.

It taught me one thing though: The wisest men say the simplest things. Simply.

Pritish Nandy
11 July 2013

THE FIRST DRAFT OF THIS TRANSLATION, I prefer to call it a version, was completed in 1977 when I was still some years away from stepping into my thirties. It would not have been possible to do it without my friend and a much older, wiser scholar Prithvinath Shastri who came into my life suddenly in the late sixties and vanished as suddenly in the early eighties when I left Calcutta to take up a job in Bombay. Bombay is no longer Bombay. Nor is Calcutta, Calcutta. After a couple of years of staying in touch intermittently from Santiniketan, where I got his letters from, Shastriji simply disappeared from my life.

During the years I knew Shastriji, who I first met at an adda at P. Lal's Writers Workshop on a balmy Sunday morning, he persuaded me to occasionally set aside my own writing and wade through the Sanskrit classics. Just for discipline, he would argue. No, not the huge tomes but the Upanishads, the Bhagavad Gita. And, most delightful of all, lots of erotic poems which may no longer look so erotic today but remain enchanting poetry nevertheless. Many of these he helped me translate and then, as life took me towards other persuasions, I forgot all about it. There was a life to be lived and other things to write and publish, and I got caught up with them.

Recently, while shifting residence in Bombay, I rediscovered these manuscripts, though over the years some of the pages had disappeared. I went back to the originals and tried to fill in the gaps and,

For Ashis, my friend, my brother, a noble man . . .

ageless at 76 in a world fast ageing . . .

Seagull Books, 2014

The designer would like to thank Naveen Kishore, Bishan Samaddar and Sandeep Banerjee for the generous use of their photographs

ISBN 978 0 85742 182 1

British Library Cataloguing-in-Publication Data
A catalogue record for this book is available from the British Library

Designed by Sunandini Banerjee, Seagull Books, Calcutta, India
Printed and bound by Hyam Enterprises
at Fotoscan Graphics Pvt Ltd, Calcutta, India

Isha Upanishad

TRANSLATED BY PRITISH NANDY
ILLUSTRATED BY SUNANDINI BANERJEE

Seagull Books
LONDON NEW YORK CALCUTTA